AWESOME NATURE

OCEANS

by K.C. Kelley

AMICUS

fish

coral reef

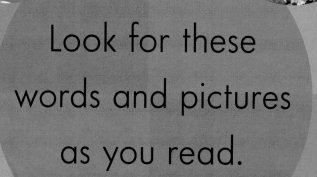

Look for these
words and pictures
as you read.

surfer

crabs

What is that?
It's the ocean!
Let's dive in!

Oceans cover most of
Earth's surface.
They are filled with saltwater.

fish

Look at the fish.
Fish live in the ocean.
Some fish swim in
groups called schools.

crabs

See the crabs?
They live at the bottom
of the ocean.
Crabs have two big claws.

coral reef

Look at the coral reef.

Reefs grow in oceans.

Many ocean animals live there.

surfer

Look at the surfer.
She rides a big wave.
Surf's up!

Megan and Luke had fun!
Another great day
at the ocean.

fish

coral reef

Did you find?

surfer

crabs

spot

Amicus Readers and Amicus Ink are imprints of Amicus
P.O. Box 1329, Mankato, MN 56002
www.amicuspublishing.us

Library of Congress Cataloging-in-Publication Data
Names: Kelley, K. C., author.
Title: Oceans / by K.C. Kelley.
Description: Mankato, MN : Amicus, [2018] | Series: Spot.
  Awesome nature | "Spot is an imprint of Amicus."
Identifiers: LCCN 2017022321 (print) | LCCN 2017033778
  (ebook) | ISBN 9781681513287 (pdf) | ISBN 9781681512884
  (library binding : alk. paper) | ISBN 9781681522487 (pbk. :
  alk. paper)
Subjects: LCSH: Ocean--Juvenile literature. | Readers (Primary)
  | Vocabulary.
Classification: LCC GC21.5 (ebook) | LCC GC21.5 .K44 2018
  (print) | DDC 551.46--dc23
LC record available at https://lccn.loc.gov/2017022321

Printed in China

HC 10 9 8 7 6 5 4 3 2 1
PB 10 9 8 7 6 5 4 3 2 1

Megan Peterson, editor
Deb Miner, series designer
Patty Kelley, book designer
Producer/Photo Research:
Shoreline Publishing Group LLC

Photos:
Cover: Asther Lau Choon
Siew/Dreamstime.com.
Inside: Dreamstime.com:
Sanga Park 1, Seaphotoart
2tl, 10, Irochka 2tr, Chris
Van Lennep 2bl, Christopher
Putnam 2br, Vadim
Khomyakov 3, Olga Topp
4, Richard Brooks 6, Budda
8, Trubavin 12, Alexander
Shalamov 14.

OCEANS